Pain, Peace
and Prayer
Lines about Loss, Life and Love

Brian D. Eyre

I0087715

**Swinging Cats and Blinking Hats Press
Dallas, Texas**

PAIN, PEACE AND PRAYER - Lines about Loss, Life and Love

Swinging Cats and Blinking Hats Press
www.swingingcatsandblinkinghats.com

Table of Contents

PASSIONATE LOVE

PAINFUL HEARTS

PERMANENT ENDINGS

PRECIOUS FAMILY

Some say that dysfunctional families are all dysfunctional in a different way, but that functional families are all the same. This section focuses on the lives of families both functional and dysfunctional. Both types are fascinating and unique, but it isn't easy to tell the difference.

One Day Sober

My momma told Daddy back in fifty-four,
"Either quit the bottle or I hit the door."
Daddy's love for Momma ran true and deep
So he made a vow that he tried hard to keep.
It was a damn hard promise to live up to;
He knew what to do.
One day, he hit his knees and began to pray
And asked God to keep him sober one more day.

He said, "Lord, don't let true love die young.
And don't let my wife see me get drunk.
If You'll let me live to be one day older,
I'll try like Hell to make it one day sober."

The doctor told Daddy back in sixty-four,
"Your youngest little boy is at death's door."
A baby who's sick is the devil's to use
To walk back in with a bottle of booze.
But Daddy loved Momma, and he loved me too,
He knew what to do.
One day, he hit his knees and began to pray
And God and Momma kept the devil away.

He said, "Lord, don't let my boy die young.
And don't let my kids see me get drunk.
If You'll let my baby get one day older,
I'll try like Hell to make it one day sober."

The devil told me back in eighty-four,
"Drink this bottle and I'll get you one more."
Now an apple won't fall very far from the tree.
And the devil sure knew how to get to me.
But I loved my family and they loved me too,
I knew what to do.
One day, I hit my knees and I began to pray
And asked God to keep me sober one more day.

Lord I'm thankful that I didn't die young
And that I never saw my daddy get drunk.
If You will let me get just one day older,
I'll try like Hell to make it one day sober.

When You Knelt to Pray

From the morning I was born, until the night you died
You were always asking God to keep me in His sight.
You prayed for all your children, as good mothers do.
But I needed your prayers the most, as you always knew.

As an infant with an illness that no child had survived,
Your constant prayers for me are what kept me alive.
Doctors treated my disease and gave me shots every day.
But I lived because God answered when you knelt to pray.

From the morning I was born, until the night you died
You were always asking God to keep me in His sight.
You prayed for all your children, as good mothers do.
But I needed your prayers the most, as you always knew.

With a breaking heart, too much speed and not a bit of thought,
I just drove almost thru a solid post in a Mercury I'd bought.
A seatbelt alone will not protect a fool who drives that way.
I only lived because God answered when you knelt to pray.

From the morning I was born, until the night you died
You were always asking God to keep me in His sight.
You prayed for all your children, as good mothers do.
But I needed your prayer the most, as you always knew.

Your prayers were always there when somebody needed help.
You always asked God's help for others, never for yourself.
I am living now the life I live, because of your unselfish way.
How I wish now you'd thought of you, when you knelt to pray.

From the instant I was born, and even since you've died
You are always asking God to keep me in His sight.
You pray for all God's children, as saints and angels do.
But I still need your prayers the most, as you always knew.

Give Your Keys to Jesus

You just can't get through Heaven's gate,
By going to your church each week,
Or by saying a nice blessing
Every time you sit to eat.
You can't just quote Bible verses
To know you'll get past heaven's door.
These things are nice, but to be saved
You must give Jesus one thing more.

Give your keys to Jesus and let your savior drive.
Give your keys to Jesus; let Him give you the ride.
Give your keys to Jesus; and He will save your soul.
Give your keys to Jesus to get where you should go.

You can't show faith in Jesus by
Treating Him like a hitchhiker.
You have to put your trust in Him
And ask Him to be your driver.
You can't ask Him to ride along
While you cling to the steering wheel.
You have to ride along with Him
While He takes you to what is real.

Give your keys to Jesus and let your savior drive.
Give your keys to Jesus; let Him give you the ride.
Give your keys to Jesus; and He will save your soul.
Give your keys to Jesus to get where you should go.

I've taken so many wrong turns
With Jesus right there by my side;
It's only because of His love
That He is still willing to drive.
I'd never make it to Heaven
Steering my life the way I do.
But Jesus will turn it around
To be sure that I make it through.

Gave my keys to Jesus and let my savior drive.
Gave my keys to Jesus; let Him give me the ride.
Gave my keys to Jesus and He will save my soul.
Gave my keys to Jesus to get where I should go.

Once

Once I posed for a photograph
I think it was in ninety three
Because my pictures on your walls
No longer looked liked me.

My hairline had receded much
Since the last time I had sat.
I'd always hated being shot
And you respected that.

Once, though I decided
To pose for a photograph.
I sat there at the mall for you.
For a portrait I could wrap.

You said it was the best gift
Of all that you'd received.
Only a mother would say that,
And only a son would believe.

Once I posed for a photograph
Which brought to you some joy.
A man I was, posing there,
Like I was still your little boy.

A gift that cost me so little
And yet you held so dear.
And somehow I only gave it,
That once in all your years.

Sonnet 123

One small boy truly blessed to be alive;
Two older siblings always by my side,
Three children trying to learn wrong from right,
We broke some rules, but we chose not to fight.

My sister worked hard at all that she tried.
My brother and I tried just to get by,
Three teens just trying to prepare for life.
We broke some rules, but we chose not to fight.

She's with her husband; he's with his wife
I'm not alone with them all by my side.
Three adults each with a different life,
And through it all, we still choose not to fight.

As parents prepare their children for life,
My wish is each one will choose not to fight.

For Better or for Worse

As soon as we were old enough
To even barely understand,
Mom took us kids every Sunday
To a church at Main and Grand.

Before I even finished school,
The city tore that old church down.
Either for better or for worse,
There's a mall there now.

Things aren't changing for the better;
And things aren't changing for the worse.
Things are changing because things change,
Be it a blessing or a curse.

As soon as I was old enough
To get myself a fake I.D.,
I took my girl every Friday
To a nightclub on Spring Valley.

Before I ever married her,
The police shut that nightclub down.
Either for better or for worse,
There's a church there now.

Things aren't changing for the better;
And things aren't changing for the worse.
Things are changing because things change,
Be it a blessing or a curse.

As soon as they are old enough
To even barely understand,
We'll take our kids every Sunday
To a church to hear God's plan.

We know what really matters most
Isn't if they tear that church down;
Either for better or for worse,
It's what they learn now.

Unforgiven

Everybody loved you, until we learned what you are.
But the love that we felt doesn't carry that far.
Some may forgive you for the sin that you chose,
But some of us can't because we loved you the most.

Jesus said he could forgive you for most any sin.
But you should not expect that from family and friends.
Jesus said we should love the sinner, while hating the sin.
And we try to do so, but we can't let you back in.

Your sin hurt your victim more than she'll ever know,
But the pain you caused us will continue to grow.
You taught us the difference between wrong and right,
But you must have forgot it over the course of time.

Jesus said he could forgive you for most any sin.
But you should not expect that from family and friends.
Jesus said we should love the sinner in spite of the sin.
And we'll try to do so, but we don't know when.

Your sin's hurting us more than it ever hurt you.
We may never again know the right thing to do
We thought you taught us what was right and wrong,
Now we find out you didn't know all along.

Jesus said we should forgive you for most any sin.
But we don't believe we can ever trust you again..
Jesus said we should love the sinner, while hating the sin.
In order to do so, must we let you back in?

Paradise by the Dashboard Lights

I've been sober now for nine years,
But those liquor stores still call me.
Changing stations and shifting gears,
I need a preacher's voice to stall me.

The Devil tries for my trucker's soul
At least a hundred times each ride.
Truck stop tramp or shot of whiskey
To help me through a lonely night.

Those radio preachers do their part
To remind me to do what's right.
Rolling along, I hear God's word;
Paradise by the dashboard light.

True to my wife, since we said our vows,
But still a man is just a man.
The truck stop tramps can't tempt me now.
The good Lord's teaching holds my hand.

The Devil tries for my trucker's soul
At least a hundred times each ride.
Truck stop tramp or shot of whiskey
To help me through a lonely night.

Those radio preachers do their part
To remind me to do what's right.
Rolling along, I hear God's word;
Paradise by the dashboard light.

I beat the Devil, again tonight;
Paradise by the dashboard light.
The gospel rides shotgun tonight;
Paradise by the dashboard light.

Sonnet 126

One penguin, two parrots, three pair of globes;
A futon with a multicolored throw,
And glasses resting in a curio
All help reveal the love inside this home.

A friend or stranger who's not in the know
May wonder why the poet lives alone
With pictures of Paris and Monroe,
But no loved ones' faces hung in photos.

Photos aren't love, love is what I know
Like mother knitting colorful throws.
Love's one penguin, two parrots, and six globes
And glasses resting in a curio.

The strangers do not mind; friends let it go;
Loved ones may have wondered, but now they know.

Going Home, Gentle

If I tell you I'll fight for breath,
I'm afraid that I'll be lying.
I'm not as scared of being dead
As I am afraid of dying.

PASSING SHIPS

Often people one barely knows have more impact than one could have ever expected. This section contains poems about people who once barely knew each other.

Amber

With a passion like a falling angel
Trying to dance on the point of a pin,
You would always party like a rock star
Until, sadly, the party had to end.

With the face to be the next top model;
A title that we all knew you would win,
You would always play it like an all star,
Until, sadly, the games all had to end.

With your hair like the color of sunlight,
You lit up every scene you were in;
You would always live like a movie star,
Until, sadly, the movie had to end.

With a smile that drove all the boys crazy
And a body as they say, 'built for sin',
You just kept on fucking like a porn star,
Until, sadly, your life came to an end.

Farewell Party

He threw himself a farewell party
And invited all his friends.
About forty of us showed up;
Free beer sure packs them in.

He said he was going to Denver
For a job he just couldn't refuse.
He thanked us all for coming;
Called us friends he'd hate to lose.

We all told him not to be silly,
That we would all still stay in touch.
A sentiment we'd all said before,
But had never meant too much.

He laughed and sang with everyone
Until the last song had been sung.
Then he told the jokes he'd told before
Till the last dog had been hung.

Then he threw another farewell party,
Inviting friends that he called true.
All three of us showed up that night,
Which he said was quite a coup.

He said he'd meant to come out
Of the closet so long ago.
We said he might as well have;
It was nothing we didn't know.

He said he was relieved to know
That we accepted him as he was.
He had feared we would hate him,
Just the way that God does.

Then he said there was no job up north;
That he was moving there to die.
I still don't know what I should have said
As a dying friend tried not to cry.

We threw our own farewell party
After our friend was truly gone.
We agreed he'd been a true friend,
But that on one thing he was wrong.

He was right that we were still his friends
As he drew his final breath.
The secret we'd kept while he died
Would stay secret in his death.

But no God could cause such a death
Out of anything close to hate.
No god that would, could ever be
A God we should tolerate.

The death of such a gentle person
May not ever be explained.
But there's no way that a just God
Meant to cause such pain.

When they throw my farewell party,
I pray that Jesus redeems my soul,
Because I want to ask His Father
About something I need to know!

If

If I'd been born a girl, and you'd been born a boy;
How much different might things have been?
Maybe you wouldn't have thought it was okay.
Or I wouldn't have drunk to impress my friends.

Did I mumble something that gave you the wrong idea
As I lay there chewing crackers, flat out on my back?
There was no way I could stop you, helpless as I was;
Almost passed out from drinking Jack Daniels Black.

If I'd been born a girl, and you'd been born a boy
Is there a chance that it would not have happened at all?
Might my friends not have trusted you with me like that
While they drank whiskey and partied down the hall.

Would they have wondered what you were doing to me,
Or at least worried enough to sometimes check back?
There was no way I could stop you, helpless as I was;
Almost passed out from drinking Jack Daniels Black.

If I'd been born a girl, and you'd been born a boy
Would I still have forgiven you, but not forgiven myself?
These are a few questions that I know I can never answer,
But I do understand why most women never tell.

Yearbook

I read the yearbook that I've ignored for years
Not to reminisce and not to shed false tears.

I simply came across it, after I thought it gone.
So now I read the notes written to say 'so long'.

'So long' is not what they say, but instead 'goodbye'.
We never did stay in touch, nor did we really try.

"Hey, you're the greatest…"   "…I'm so glad we met."
"Friends forever and…"   "…that I'll never forget."
"What can be said, that…"   "… you are really neat."
"To a really great guy…" "… you are so sweet."
"Thanks for being my…" "…the good times aren't done."
"To the neatest big brother…" "…loads of fun."

I don't live in the past and I don't miss those times.
In fact, I don't recall most of the names that signed.

But I remember so well, the crush I had on one girl
To whom I meant little, though she was my world.

Two decades later, I just can't help but wonder
If I knew then why she added her phone number.

Hobo

He's a modern day hobo, but there ain't no train
Running through Dallas past Ervay and Main.
No one writes odes now to the free life he's living.
But there's a meal on Christmas and on Thanksgiving.

She spent more at Neiman's than he sees in a year,
But won't spare him a buck, scared that he'll buy beer.
As if one drink of beer might cause his undoin';
Like there's anything left in his life to be ruined.

A cell at Lew Sterrett would be a better place to stay
Than the sidewalk by this trash pile where he lives today.
But he can't even get arrested to help him survive.
Nobody will acknowledge that he is even alive.

He's a modern day hobo, but there ain't no train
Running through Dallas past Ervay and Main.
No one writes odes now to the free life he's living.
But there's a meal on Christmas and on Thanksgiving.

The news vans park on this corner in the same place,
Each time they show up with the smiling TV face.
Last time they told his tale and showed this trash pile;
Today they're just here to show Neiman's new style.

They all walk right past him as if he's not here;
Yet they still manage to step a few feet clear.
He doesn't need pity; he doesn't want prayer.
He just wants a dollar if you have one to spare.

He's a modern day hobo, but it's a damn shame
That instead of helping, we all try to fix blame.
If there's a way to improve the life he's living,
It will take twelve months, not two days of giving.

Flame

Once a mustang has been broken, if somebody treats it well,
It might in time forgive mankind for putting it through hell.

But, women aren't like horses; at least, the one you're with is not.
She won't live to forget and forgive, unless she really has forgot.

Just that you didn't start the fire won't protect you from the flame.
The blaze that has been burning long will burn you just the same.

Somebody did her wrong one time; a man who was a fool.
Now, she won't ever trust again, and you can't break a rule.

You'll sometimes find that she treats you kind, if you understand
That you always stay one step away from being just another man.

Just that you didn't start the fire won't protect you from the flame.
The blaze that has been burning long will burn you just the same.

I started that fire so long ago, that I no longer feel the flame.
The next time you get burnt by her, just know that I'm to blame.

Peace and Happiness

In this fallen world we live in,
You will always face pain.
But peace and happiness are still
Things that you can obtain.

The peace that you're seeking;
You may not ever know,
If you keep holding onto pain
That you need to let go.

You keep looking for happiness,
But it is not around
Because you are looking for it
Where it is never found.

Peace can't be found by chasing it
Or its symbolic dove.
Nor is it found by expecting
To get it from your love.

No one can buy you happiness,
Not even you, yourself.
No house or car or possession,
Can improve how you feel.

Peace can be found in the Lord Christ.
He has taught us what's true.
We should forgive our trespassers,
To be forgiven, too.

Happiness must come from within;
A heart singing its song.
It is a heart filled with this love
That will always be strong.

In this fallen world we live in,
You will always face pain.
But peace and happiness are still
Things that you can obtain.

True Friends

My first true friend said she'd leave me never.
She promised that our friendship wouldn't end.
I told her we would be friends forever.
She was my first true friend
Grade school ended, and so did junior high.
But our true friendship didn't end.
When our paths would cross we'd say hi,
Since we were still true friends.

We both graduated twenty years ago.
If I even miss her now, I don't know.

My best true friend took me under his wing,
Taught me to be cool or at least pretend.
He was a big star, at everything.
I was too, as his friend.
He got drafted in the eleventh round.
I drove him to airport terminal D.
He waved as the plane left the ground.
His games were on t.v.

We quit staying in touch ten years ago.
If I even miss those days, I don't know.

My next true friend I haven't really met.
But she is my true friend here on MySpace.
We've had no bad fights to later regret,
Nor good times to embrace.
We'll get around to it one of these days.
Either I'll invite her somewhere to meet,
Or she'll invite me and I'll say, 'okay'.
Then true friends, we will be.

You never know how a friendship will go;
We might become bff's, I don't know.

If I Had

You made no effort to know me,
So I made no effort to know you.
I was just working for the summer;
I presumed that you were too.

You seemed like a decent guy,
But I didn't know if you were cool.
So I hung with my old friends;
You weren't even from our school.

We wondered about you,
But we gave little thought to your acts.
There were always rumors,
But we knew that rumors are not facts.

Then you just weren't there,
And all the gossip came to the front.
Were you shot, were you in jail,
Had you moved back to Vermont?

Then the rumors turned into truth;
You were lying in a hospital bed.
You had taken a twenty-two rifle
And put a bullet in your head.

You seemed like a decent guy,
But I'd never really been your friend.
If I had been, wouldn't I have known
You were this close to the end?

The Actress

I am working as an actress, doing my best to play my part.
I didn't get to write the script, but I know all my lines by heart.
I wear the costume for the role, serve drinks and smile on cue.
I've only played my part just right if the men think it's true.

The cowboys who leave tips have to believe that I don't mind,
If they think my name is Honey, and check out my behind.
They sit here every night and act like they don't have wives.
And I pretend that I might care, and we all live dishonest lives.

But I am merely an actress, playing well a challenging part.
They all think I'm a tease, but they don't know my heart.
If they knew they aren't my type, they'd pretend that it's okay,
But my tips might be so small, that I could not live on the pay.

So I pretend that I like them, as other girls might like a guy.
But the truth is that it's a role I am playing just to get by.
So I act like it doesn't hurt to hide behind this script I hate,
And wonder if I'll make it out of here before it is too late.

I can't keep being an actress; somehow I have to turn the page.
Some people call this a closet, but to me it's more of a cage.
By either name, it's a prison, and I just have to break away.
I'll never get to be myself until I tell the world that I'm gay.

Laundry Room

You're blinded by sight so you don't see me at all.
I hear you tiptoe around me hoping that I won't hear.
I'm not crippled by vision so I see just who you are.
You can't walk soft enough to just disappear.

I'm not a beggar or leper, and I'm not a pariah;
But you don't even say a single word to me.
I'm just another guy waiting for a dryer.
But you wait for yours without talking to me.

You're blinded by sight so you don't see me at all.
I hear you tiptoe around me hoping that I won't hear.
I'm not crippled by vision so I see just who you are.
You can't walk soft enough to just disappear.

I caught a bad break which I try to fight through.
Bad luck took my eyes, not my voice or my ears.
It might help pass the time if I could just talk to you.
But you've judged me too soon because of your fears.

You're blinded by sight so you don't see me at all.
I hear you tiptoe around me hoping that I won't hear.
I'm not crippled by vision so I see just who you are.
You can't walk soft enough to just disappear.

I wash and dry all of my monochrome clothes.
I don't see anybody as they all do the same.
But I hear everybody that comes in or goes,
Although nobody here even knows my name.

You're blinded by sight so you don't see me at all.
I hear you tiptoe around me hoping that I won't hear.
I'm not crippled by vision so I see just who you are.
You can't walk soft enough to just disappear.

PERFECT STRANGERS

Celebrities may not make good role models, but they are barely known by millions of people and therefore, will have an impact on millions of lives. The poems in this section reveal the impact that a few of them have made or are making.

Dutch and Stanley

Dutch and Stanley have much in common;
Like being shot in 'Eighty One
By a crazy man who got his hands
On a twenty-two caliber gun.

The next thing we heard Reagan say
Was a joke about the doctor's point of view.
It was not that funny, but we all laughed,
Knowing what Reagan had gone through.

Dutch and Stanley have much in common;
Like being shot in 'Eighty One
By a crazy man who got his hands
On a twenty-two caliber gun.

The next thing we heard Stanley say
Was a joke about the use of a twenty two.
It was pretty funny, but no one laughed,
Knowing what Stanley had gone through.

They both have kept us laughing,
But Dutch is dead now at ninety three.
At least I know that if I still need a laugh,
I can always call on Stanley.

Ogden Nash

I love the words of Mister Nash
Who wrote for joy and for cash.
I have chuckled so very often
At the clever poems of Ogden,
That now I laugh about the same
When I hear his words or his name.

Dear Emily

Like you to Death two times I've paid the price.
I was with you when your life closed twice.
But I need not to wait and see
Your curséd Immortality.
I fear not what it might reveal
For twice I've died; nothing's left to kill.

The Voice of God

Driving down a silent highway,
With no radio in my truck
Praying God would show me a way
To end my pain and change my luck.
Then I heard a voice, which seemed odd
From out of the dash.
I knew it was the voice of God,
Sounding like Johnny Cash.

I listened as the voice explained
Where my life had gone in the tank.
I'd just asked God to ease my pain,
Instead of showing Him my thanks.
I understood what I'd been taught
Way back in the past.
I knew it was the voice of God
Sounding like Johnny Cash.

You too may hear His voice,
When you least expect it.
If you should get that choice,
You should not reject it.

As you drive down that long highway,
You might also receive a sign,
A song so true it guides your way
Like 'Ring of Fire" inside your mind.
Don't treat it as a passing thought,
Be sure that you grasp
That you have heard the voice of God
Sounding like Johnny Cash.

And listen to the voice of God
It sounds like Johnny Cash.

Don't Panic

Your writing reaches us inside
Just like a Vogon Poem does not.
While it might make us wish to die,
Yours teaches us new ways of thought.
You write of things insane and wise,
And people simple and absurd;
All started with some great advice;
Summed up for us in just two words.

Your character, Dent Arthur Dent
Is everyman, but one thing's odd;
Most of us who he represents
See ourselves as Ford or Zaphod
Two heads will be better than one
If we're to steal the Heart of Gold.
But if we ride with a Vogon,
We know to bring a towel to hold.

Too soon your life came to an end,
Leaving too many unwritten lines.
Was your last thought "No, not again"
Or "How am I doing for time?"
You wrote of folks insane and wise
In settings simple and absurd,
And left one piece of great advice;
Summed up for us in just two words.

Don't panic!

Sonnet 120880

Mortal men must die of mortal means,
But you seemed blessed with immortality.
With your jaded songs and faded jeans,
You seemed above the gun of lunacy.

You said you wished to die before your wife,
For without her love you could not carry on.
But what about the sorrow now in her life,
Now that she is here and you are gone.

The many who have heard your jaded song
Feel that we too died with you last night.
To us you were the one who did no wrong;
No matter what might happen, you'd make it right.

With you away, is your music all that lives
To remind us of the ways that your heart gives?

Sonnet 316

An entire nation watches your preaching.
Your dynamic style sure brings the flock in.
They all want to learn of what you're teaching
About Jesus dying for all our sins.

Your syndication is so far-reaching,
And so much praise and cash kept flowing in.
That you forgot the Word you were teaching
Of how only Jesus was without sin.

The congregation that you are fleecing
Keeps writing checks and sending them in.
The moneychangers that Christ sent fleeing
Were what you have become now: Benny Hinn.

So you've no right to tell us what to do,
And we won't be sending our tithes to you.

Redneck Time Machine

Hey, Mister Lincoln,
What were you thinkin'
As you left home to watch that dang ol' play?
As for you, Nero,
I'm itchin' to know
If you really fiddled that disastrous day?

Mister Henry Ford,
Can I get a word
On how you created your auto empire?
Missus O'Leary,
Please tell me, Dearie,
Just how your cow started that big ol' fire?

And for Neil and Buzz,
My one question was,
What was it like walking there on the moon?
For He on the cross,
My saviour and boss,
Please tell me, will You be coming back soon?

Don't Have to Die

If you want to be an Outlaw, you gotta break some rules.
If you want to be like Possum, you gotta need that bottle.
If you want to be true country, you can't care if it's cool.
Or else, it will all sound hollow.

You don't have to die to be Hank Williams,
But you sure as Hell have to live.
You need to love a girl with all your heart,
But make mistakes she won't forgive.
You don't have to die to be Hank Williams,
But you sure as Hell have to feel.
So when you pour your pain into each song,
The whole world knows it's real.

To be like the Singing Cowboy, you gotta hit the trail.
To be like the Texas Playboys, you gotta have that swing.
To be like the Storyteller, you need a story to tell.
Or else, it just won't mean a thing.

You don't have to die to be Hank Williams,
But you sure as Hell have to live.
You need to love a girl with all your heart,
But make mistakes she won't forgive.
You don't have to die to be Hank Williams,
But you sure as Hell have to feel.
So when you pour your pain into each song,
The whole world knows it's real.

To be a Son of the Pioneers, you gotta ride the range.
To become like the Man in Black, you gotta go to prison.
To be like the King of the Road, you gotta hop a train,
Or else, nobody will listen.

You don't have to die to be Hank Williams,
But you sure as Hell have to live.
You need to love a girl with all your heart,
But make mistakes she won't forgive.
You don't have to die to be Hank Williams,
But you sure as Hell have to feel.
So when you pour your pain into each song,
The whole world knows it's real.

I don't have to die to be Hank Williams,
But I'm still gonna have to die.
That's why I pour my pain into each song
I sing, so they won't see me cry.

PROUD HOME

It is said that it is not logical to take pride in one's place of birth. The people who say that must not have been born in Texas. This section contains poems which express the pride associated with being an American by birth and a Texan by the Grace of God.

That's How I Feel

I'll choose a Chevy any day.
Those other trucks will never do.
I'll always want a Chevrolet,
And that's how I feel about you.

True to my school, I'll always be.
Not just a school, a point of view.
Nothing could change my loyalty,
And that's how I feel about you.

I'll never change my brand of beer;
Shiner Boch is my only brew.
I love its taste; it brings me cheer,
And that's how I feel about you.

Five Super Bowls that I've enjoyed
Were won by the Silver and Blue.
I repeat, 'How 'bout them Cowboys'?
And that's how I feel about you.

Honor will last for those who died,
As those at the Alamo knew.
I'm Texas born with Texas pride.
And that's how I feel about you.

Great country singers that I know
Sing songs that are timeless and true,
Like Bob Wills or like Bill Monroe.
And that's how I feel about you.

The Marine's motto, 'Semper Fi';
It means that the proud and the few
Are honor bound to fight and die,
And that's how I feel about you.

To your sweet love, I'd remain true,
Even if you would set me free.
You know how I feel about you,
Is that how you feel about me?

Home Again, Pt. 1

She is not like other lovers;
She'll forgive you for where you've been.
Even when you flirt with others,
She'll welcome you back home again.

If you go back because you missed her,
Her rival's loss will be her gain.
But if you go back when you've been scorned,
She will ease your pain.

You weren't the first to leave her
And not the first one to return.
It seems that all her lovers
Have lessons they must learn.

She's the lady they call Texas,
She'll forgive you for where you've been.
Even though you flirt with others,
She'll welcome you back home again.

Robert Earl went to Cashville,
Like Willie and Waylon and Kris.
Those outlaws could have warned him,
Nothing good would come of this.

They told him how to dress and sing;
How to walk and wear his hair.
They took the boy away from Texas,
But they could not keep him there.

He was lured by false promises
And undelivered charms.
But each lover that leaves Texas,
Will soon be back in her arms.

She's the lady they call Texas,
She'll forgive you for where you've been.
Even though you flirt with others
She'll welcome you back home again.

Tommy Lee went to HollowWood
For a mistress they call fame.
But he learned like many others
Even the winners lose that game.

So he took the money that he earned
And bought himself a farm.
And like she has with all the others,
Texas took him in her arms.

He was lured by false promises
And undelivered charms.
But each lover that leaves Texas
Will soon be back in her arms.

She's the lady they call Texas,
She'll forgive you for where you've been.
Even though you flirt with others
She'll welcome you back home again.

She's the lady they call Texas.
You carry part of her within.
Wherever you may travel,
You can come home again.

Five Heroes

He said he'd bring a medal home
From the war, so she'd be proud.
He said he'd lead the parade
Through town and play the bugle loud.

He said the war would soon be done,
And she'd have a hero for a son.
But wars don't end, till they all fall,
And now she has no son at all.

They sent the medals home
With a letter saying she should be proud.
But when the parade goes marching by,
He won't play the bugle loud.

For him the war's already done,
And she's got a hero, not a son.
Cause your war ends when you fall,
And now she has no son at all.

She put the medals with his dad's;
She stares at them, but feels not proud.
She sits around the house all day
And plays her radio too loud.

She thought the wars would soon be done,
And she'd have a husband and a son.
But wars don't end, till the last ones fall,
And now she has no one at all.

Now she knows the reasons why
Her mother never seemed that proud.
Why she had flags on closet shelves,
And played her Victrola too loud.

She knows that war is never done
To someone who has lost a son.
But wars don't end, till they all fall
And now she has no son at all.

She knows that flags on closet shelves
Do not make a woman proud.
They only make her want to cry,
And play the music way too loud.

She knows that wars will not be done
As long as someone has a son
Or daughter now to fight and fall,
And now she has no child at all.

Time Warp

On a bus going nowhere, nowhere to go and going there fast,
I met an old man of many years, and this looked to be his last.
When he first started talking, I thought he'd lost his head.
But it started to make sense as I heard the words he said.

I'm telling you his story just as he told it to me.
I suggest that you not judge until you listen carefully.
"I'm drinking rum and coca cola in nineteen forty-five,
While cursing the Ayatollah wishing he were not alive.

I live in a time warp; the dates and times get lost.
I wish I could stay home, but I can't afford the cost."
His eyes were full of tears and his voice was just a buzz.
I interrupted him to ask if he knew where he was.

He said, "I know where I'm at, I never forget that, man.
But I sometimes forget when, or just don't give a damn.
If I had any money, boy, they would all think I was well.
If Harry S. was here right now, he'd surely give them hell.

Whippersnapper, everybody loves you now, but in a while,
You'll be the man I am now; you'll know you're not senile.
I'll be gone, and you will be the one in my shoes.
Nobody will care that you're alone with the blues.

You will be asking not to be put away.
And no one will care what you have to say."
I said, "It's been nice to meet you, but this is my stop."
As I stepped off the bus I heard him give a small cough.

And say, "Nobody will care what you have to say,
Goodbye, young man, we are both going away.
I'm drinking rum and coca cola in nineteen forty-five,
While cursing out Osama wishing he were not alive.

I live in a time warp; the dates and times get lost.
I wish I could stay home, but I can't afford the cost."
I read in the paper the following day,
"Old man riding bus, passes away."

Pre-Occupied

The union met with the company man;
Said we wanted raises and took a stand.
The damn company said not any more,
And then sent all our jobs to Singapore.
Now I work at two jobs for half the pay
That we scoffed at 'til they took it away.
Half what I made isn't nearly enough
To keep me from having to pawn my stuff.

I could protest corporate greed; hold up signs 'til my fingers bleed.
But I know the truth is that wouldn't help.
I could curse at the president; demand help from the government.
But I know the truth and I blame myself.

The union says I shouldn't take this choice,
But I don't see why it should have a voice.
I might not be here at minimum wage,
If the damn union hadn't turned the page,
By demanding too much pay from the man.
Now, I have to work wherever I can.
Take what they give and try to make ends meet;
Knowing I'm headed down a dead end street.

I could protest the union's greed; hold up signs 'til my fingers bleed.
But I know the truth is that wouldn't help.
I could curse at the president; demand help from the government.
But I know the truth and I blame myself.

We fill up the tanks in our SUVs,
And blame the price on the oil companies.
We buy Hondas, Nissans, and Toyotas,
While we blame the debt on General Motors.
We try to buy more house than we can ever own.
Then we blame the bank that financed our loan.
We try to get rich in a Ponzi scheme,
Then we blame all the Fat Cats on Wall Street.

Now we riot in the streets, pretend that we Occupy Wall Street
But we know the truth is that it won't help.
We're cursing at the president; burning down the government.
But if we face the truth, we'll blame ourselves.

Armadillos and Highway Patrol

It's a five hour drive down I-35
From Cowtown to San Antonio.
I have time to unload and get back on the road;
No time to see the Alamo.

There're sights all around in each Texas town,
But I've no time to see them as I roll.
As I speed right by, what catches my eye
Are armadillos and Highway Patrol.
Two Eighty Seven North, on up from Fort Worth;
Just me, my truck and Charley Pride.
The cascades aren't small in Wichita Falls,
But there's no time for that on this ride.

Hopped up on Bennie; eastbound on Twenty
From Fort Worth to Texarkana,
There's no time for fun at the end of this run
In the casinos of Louisiana.

There're sights all around in each Texas town,
But I've no time to see them as I roll.
As I speed right by, what catches my eye
Are armadillos and Highway Patrol.
Two Eighty Seven North, on up from Fort Worth;
Just me, my truck and Charley Pride.
The cascades aren't small in Wichita Falls,
But there's no time for that on this ride.

It's a four hour drive down I-45
From the Metroplex to Houston.
It's so fun to play on the Galveston Bay;
No time for that on this run.

There're sights all around in each Texas town,
But I've no time to see them as I roll.
As I speed right by, what catches my eye
Are armadillos and Highway Patrol.
Two Eighty Seven North, on up from Fort Worth;
Just me, my truck and Charley Pride.
The cascades aren't small in Wichita Falls,
But there's no time for that on this ride.

Deadheading my Kenworth back home to Fort Worth;
Just me, my truck and Robert Earl.
Not making a dime, but I'm making good time
As I speed home to be with my girl.
There're sights all around in each Texas town,
But not one could ever come close
To the love that I see in the eyes that love me
Of the girl whose love means the most.

Home Again, Pt. 2

I am not like other lovers;
I forgive you for where you've been.
Even though you flirt with others,
I welcome you back home again.

If you're back because you missed me,
I hope her loss will be my gain.
But if you're back because she scorned you,
I am here to ease your pain.

You weren't the first to leave me
And not the first one to return.
It seems that all my lovers
Have lessons they must learn.

I'm the lady they call Texas;
I forgive you for where you've been.
Even though you flirt with others,
I welcome you back home again.

Janis Lyn went up to Drugstock,
And she did most everything.
If only she had realized
All she needed was to sing.

But I forgive her trespasses,
And I won't judge her sins.
Like all my other lovers,
She is welcome back again.

She was lured by false promises
And undelivered charms.
It took me too long to forgive her,
But I now hold her in my arms.

I'm the lady they call Texas;
I forgive you for where you've been.
Even though you flirt with others,
I welcome you back home again.

Natalie went to the other Paris,
And told the world she was ashamed.
It cut me deep to hear her say that,
But I'll forgive her just the same.

It's easy to forget your roots
After you've conquered the world.
But I will always think of her as
Just Lloyd Maines' little girl.

She was lured with false promises
And undelivered charms.
I'll forgive her when she wants me to,
And welcome her back in my arms.

I'm the lady they call Texas.
You carry part of me within.
Wherever you may travel,
You can come home again.

PAINTED TOWNS

Young people often paint the town red. All of us were young once, and some of us still are. This section contains poems about the different ways there are to paint the town. Red is not the only color that a town can be painted.

Good Kind of Pain

We once were weekend warriors with a will to win;
On the field to chase trophies, not there to make friends.
We lived by the motto, 'Hit it hard, then run fast,
And play each game like it's your last."

We would get home with scars and with blood on our shirts
From taking dives after line drives on rock hard dirt.
Since winning is what mattered when playing ball games,
We called it a good kind of pain.

We were honky-tonk heroes in our favorite bars,
Drinking whiskey until we couldn't find our cars.
We lived by the motto, "Party hard and drink fast
And live each day like it's your last."

We would get home being glad to not be in jail,
Then we would wake up with headaches that hurt like hell.
Since we didn't mind losing at those drinking games,
We called it a good kind of pain.

I'm older I know and wiser I hope,
A few things about me have changed.
And the one thing new, I know to be true
Is there is no good kind of pain.

A casual Casanova on those youthful nights,
I fell in and out of love at the speed of light.
I lived by the motto, "Fuck her hard, then leave fast,
And love each girl like she's my last."

I would get home alone and try hard to believe
That one night stands were all I planned, and all I need.
Since leaving isn't winning when love is the game,
Can't call it a good kind of pain.

Heaven in a Glass

I was living a real good life;
A great career and lovely wife;
A big house with a swimming pool,
And two children in private schools.

I drove a brand new luxury car
And ate the finest caviar.
I always had money to spend;
I never dreamed that life might end.

Once I heard a society woman say
With a tone of voice that revealed her class,
That a Sonoma Valley Chardonnay
Is heaven in a glass.

Now I hear the voice of the good man,
With a free meal for us and the Bible,
Tell me the wine that is now in my hand
Is hell in a bottle.

Now I just barely have a life,
I lost my children and my wife.
They left me when I lost my mind
And became a slave to the wine.

Now I live off handouts and think
About how to get one more drink.
With no money for me to spend,
I only dream this life will end.

Once I heard a society woman say,
With a tone of voice that revealed her class,
That a Sonoma Valley Chardonnay
Is heaven in a glass.

Now I hear the voice of the good man,
With a free meal for us and the Bible,
Tell me the wine that is now in my hand
Is hell in a bottle.

I pray that I'll find peace one day,
With my sins being washed away
By our Savior's forgiving grace;
Leaving no desire for wine's taste.

But until then I'll live in shame,
Knowing that I have caused such pain.
But I've learned one thing from my past:
You can't find heaven in a glass.

Once I heard a society woman say,
With a tone of voice that revealed her class,
That a Sonoma Valley Chardonnay
Is heaven in a glass.

Now I hear the voice of the good man,
With a free meal for us and the Bible,
Tell me the wine that is now in my hand
Is hell in a bottle.

If I'm to find Heaven at last,
I know it won't be in a glass!

When Did I Grow Up?

It's been years since the last time that I chased fireflies
Or made little fortresses out of my French fries.
Now, I know there are no monsters under my bed,
And that the airplanes won't run into Santa's sled.

I knew, of course, that I'd get old,
Nobody stays a pup.
But one thing that I'd like to know
Is "When did I grow up?"

It's been years since I've gotten into a fistfight
Or been caught skinny-dipping under the moonlight.
Now, those drag strip car races aren't part of my plan,
Since I replaced my hotrod with a safe sedan.

I knew, of course, that I'd get old.
Nobody stays a pup.
But one thing that I'd like to know
Is "When did I grow up?"

It's been years since the last time I closed down a bar
Or called a cab because I couldn't find my car.
Now, when I do drink, I make sure I stay sober,
So I don't wake up with a migraine hangover.

I knew, of course, that I'd get old,
Nobody stays a pup.
But one thing that I'd like to know
Is "When did I grow up?"

One more thing that I'd like to know
Is "Why did I have to grow up?"
I know that I had to grow old,
But I never meant to grow up.

Beer Drinking Man

I don't smoke and I don't gamble.
In fact, my only vice
Is the one I keep in my truck:
A cold six-pack on ice.

I'm a hard working, clean living, beer drinking man.
I don't drink as much as I want
I just drink what I can.
I'm a hard working, clean living, beer drinking man.
I am the way I've always been.
No change is in my plan.

I don't hit on any waitresses,
I'd never cheat on you.
Nothing wrong with a working man
Enjoying a cold brew.

I'm a hard working, clean living, beer drinking man.
I don't drink as much as I want,
I just drink what I can.
I'm a hard working, clean living, beer drinking man.
I am the way I've always been.
No change is in my plan.

If you can't live with who I am,
Then you can't live with me.
If that's the way you really feel,
Then you should set me free.

I'm a hard working, clean living, beer drinking man.
I don't drink as much as I want,
I just drink what I can.
I'm a hard working, clean living, beer drinking man.
I am the way I've always been.
No change is in my plan.

I'm a hard working, clean living, beer drinking man.
I don't drown problems in bottles;
I like my beer in cans.
I'm a hard working, clean living, beer drinking man.

Number One Song

You say if I try that I could stop it,
Every fight's because I drank a brew.
But all that's being tried is my patience;
All I'm trying to stop right now is you.

You say I shouldn't listen to my friends.
That I should be listening to my heart.
And so I'm listenin', but it's not missin'
You when we're apart.

If you'd quit thinking
I should quit drinking;
Maybe we could learn to get along.
There's less chance of that
Than the chances that,
This song will be a number one song.

When I open my mouth you start fighting,
You just assume that I must be lying.
When I leave the house you think I'm cheating.
When I just go out to keep from crying.

It only takes just one bottle of beer
To give you something we can fight about.
I'd go to prison to never listen
To you when you shout.

If you'd quit thinking
I should quit drinking;
Maybe we could learn to get along.
There's less chance of that
Than the chances that,
This song will be a number one song.

You don't like any of my good buddies,
And I don't much like your momma either.
I like my bird dogs more than I like you,
And you don't like none of them, neither.

When I see a plane or an Amtrack train,
I always wish like hell I was on board.
But fares don't come cheap, so when I do leave,
It'll be in my Ford.

If you'd quit thinking
I should quit drinking;
Maybe we could learn to get along.
That just won't happen;
You'll just keep naggin',
Until this becomes a number one song.

Companion

I don't miss my old companion much,
But I miss how we fought the blues.
I don't miss what we did so much
As the freedom we had to choose.
Back then I called her loneliness,
Now I know her as Miss Liberty.
I never dreamed forsaking her,
Would be the cause of any misery.

I thought that I was lonely then,
But I was simply not aware.
That we could do most anything
Without a single care.
We got kicked out of honky-tonks
In at least four states,
Doing things that we would never do,
If we were out on dates.

In New Orleans for Mardi Gras,
We were drinking Huge Ass Beer;
An unsafe place for smart mouthed
Light-weights, but we had no fear.
In Austin down on Sixth Street,
Aiming for a drink at every bar;
We had a hell of a time trying,
Although we didn't make it far.

I don't miss my old companion much,
But I miss how we fought the blues.
I don't miss what we did so much
As the freedom we had to choose.
Back then I called her loneliness,
Now I know her as Miss Liberty.
I never dreamed forsaking her,
Would be the cause of any misery.

We argued with a bouncer
At a club just west of Hurst.
A fight that might have lasted,
If he had not hit me first.
I don't know why he did that,
We were just having a little fun.
Maybe looking for someone to hit,
And I turned out to be the one.

Being together is by far better
Than alone could ever be.
But I still miss Miss Liberty
And wonder if she misses me.
This doesn't mean our love's not right
Or that you aren't the one.
Just that some days I miss the nights
When crazy passed for fun.

Texas Hold'em

Playing poker on Tuesday nights;
I can't believe it caused our fight.
Staring down at the cards tonight,
I think you may be right.

One winning hand won't make a rich man
But one goodbye sure made me cry.
I cried a little about the river.
I cried a lot with every flop.
Pocket aces can cause sad faces,
Only my heart's not in these cards.
I cried a little about the river
I cried a lot with every flop.

I'll call to tell you I'm staying.
There's no way that we should fold 'em.
It depends on how I play it,
Like in Texas Hold 'em.

One winning hand won't make a rich man
But one goodbye sure made me cry.
I cried a little about the river.
I cried a lot with every flop.

Pocket aces can cause sad faces,
Only my heart's not in these cards.
I cried a little about the river
I cried a lot with every flop.

You know that when push comes to shove,
It's true sometimes we can't all win.
But when it comes to your true love,
I'll always be all in!
One winning hand won't make a rich man
But one goodbye sure made me cry.
I cried a little about the river.
I cried a lot with every flop.

Pocket aces can cause sad faces,
Only my heart's not in these cards.
I cried a little about the river
I cried a lot with every flop.

Pocket aces, so I'm all in. A bad beat; I'm bust and done.
Now I'm coming home to the best hand that I've ever won.

Poor Me

I never had the strength to give up any vice.
Being poor is the only thing keeping me alive.
It limits my consumption and the damage I could do,
If I had the money to party the whole night through.

Welcome

We still like the party crowd.
We like to get wild and loud.
But we've worn out our welcome
All around Deep Ellum.

They've banned us still
Up and down Greenville.
They don't let us go
Down to Restaurant Row.

They don't want us around
All the bars uptown.
They just won't let us in
The pubs in the West End

We still like the party crowd
We like to get wild and loud.
So come over any night,
We party here all the time.

Tournaments

It's not whether we win or lose; it's whether we win, place or show.
If we don't leave with 'hardware', its just practice, don't you know?

Some weekends are 'Nothing Special', but some are 'Nuff Sedd'.
Just take it easy on the umpires, whether they wear blue or red.

It's not whether we win or lose; it's whether we win, place or show.
If we don't leave with 'hardware', it's just practice, don't you know?

Whether its to San Antone, Austin, Tulsa or Ardmore,
it's always worth the travel time, if we win three or four.

It's not whether we win or lose; it's whether we win, place or show.
If we don't leave with 'hardware', it's just practice, don't you know?

Some times we play all weekend, sometimes it's 'two and through'.
At least if we're out early, that leaves the whole day free for brew.

It's not whether we win or lose; it's whether we win, place or show.
If we don't leave with 'hardware', it's just practice, don't you know?

Picnic league? I'm getting in my swings with my new bat.
You'll never catch me sandbagging, I'm just not into that.

It's not whether we win or lose; it's whether we win, place or show.
If we don't leave with 'hardware', it's just practice, don't you know?

PASSIONATE LOVE

The best moments in life and the worst moments in life are always a result of being in love. This section is mostly about the relationships that lead to those best moments.

That Was Then

There's a distant look in your eyes,
That look you get when we must part.
It's that sad look I recognize
Means that you fear I'll break your heart.
You're thinking that I'll be untrue.
But, it's just him you're thinking of.
I won't do what he did to you.
That was then; this is love!

When we talk on the telephone,
I hear the sadness in your voice.
You just can't stand to be alone,
Although we often have no choice.
You're thinking that I want to leave,
But it's just him you're thinking of.
What can I say so you'll believe
That was then; this is love?

Our love is perfect when we're together,
And I won't break my vow.
But, if we're to live happily ever after,
You must live in the now.

I see you cry yourself to sleep
And wonder what the Hell to do.
I know the cuts he made were deep,
Why can't you see I'm here for you?
You're thinking that I might leave you,
But it's just him you're thinking of.
I won't do what he did to you.
That was then; this is love!

That was him; this is us.
That was then; this is love!

Bluebonnets

They once called them Ladybird's folly.
We should all have a folly so real.
Each spring, all the highways in Texas
Are embanked by a bluebonnet field.

All of the boys and girls get dressed up
In their finest clothes and newest shoes,
By proud parents who take their pictures
Posing there with the bluebonnet hues.

They used to say our love was folly,
Pretending it was not something real.
But our love grows on and continues,
Just like Ladybird's bluebonnet fields.

The love that we share is a real love,
As enduring as Shakespeare's sonnets.
Our love is a love that is timeless,
So much like those Texas bluebonnets.

There are those who think it is folly
To think Shakespeare wrote every line;
They say he could never have produced
So much art in a single lifetime.

But each line was written by someone
And so all the actors play their parts.
No matter who wrote Shakespeare's poems,
Each one has touched a few million hearts.

They can not say our love is folly
Or pretend it is not something real.
Since our love grows on and continues,
Just like those Texas bluebonnet fields.

The love that we share is a real love,
As enduring as Shakespeare's sonnets.
Our love is a love that is timeless,
So much like those Texas bluebonnets.

Cindy

With my arms around you as your love surrounds me,
I'm wrapped in your blonde hair where I most want to be.
As your soft lips meet my kiss, troubles all melt away.
I fall inside your deep blue eyes, where I want to stay

We play on the midway of the Fair and at Grapefest,
The games I can't win; but together we're best.
We win prize after prize, much to the surprise
Of the grizzled old carneys with wide startled eyes.

With my arms around you as your love surrounds me,
I'm wrapped in your blonde hair where I most want to be.
As your soft lips meet my kiss, troubles all melt away;
I fall inside your deep blue eyes, where I want to stay.

Your soft touch makes it much like there is no world;
What's out there can't ever scare me or my pretty girl.
Once in a while, I make you smile, then I am proud
That it's just us and our love; all alone in this crowd.

With my arms around you as your love surrounds me,
I'm wrapped in your blonde hair where I most want to be.
As your soft lips meet my kiss, troubles all melt away;
I fall inside your deep blue eyes, where I want to stay.

Honey

Sometimes I call you Pooh Bear because I want to be your honey.
Sometimes I call you Sunshine because you make my life so sunny.
Sometimes I call you Sugarpie because you sweeten up my day.
But, as long as I can call on you, I'll call you anything you say.

Sonnet 71

If I permit myself to fall for you,
I could be hurt in ways unknown to me.
Although I've suffered infidelity,
'Twas not by love I once had thought was true.

My pain when cheated by an ingénue
Compared but not to how my pain would be,
If one with your wisdom and your beauty
Were to betray my love and be untrue.

And so, I must deny the way I feel,
To keep my heart contained, and not in pain.
To give my love to you just might be real,
A risk too great, despite what might be gained.

True joy is lost for those who take no chance,
But pain is not denied by happenstance.

Nothing at All

I don't want to be the one that you text
Every time you need someone to call.
I want to be the one that you sext
Every time you wear nothing at all.

I don't want to be the place you run to
Every time you need some place to run.
I want to be the one that you find is true
When you complete your searching for the one.

Now, I love that you call me late at night
Every time you need someone to call.
Because I am the one that holds you tight
Every time you wear nothing at all.

As we walk down the aisle side by side
I smile; delighted you are now my bride,

Three Things

The only three things that I'll ever need;
The things that I hold dear
Are Grace from God, love from you
And an ice cold bottle of beer.

Yes, God made beer to prove His love
To me and all mankind,
And God made you to prove to me
That true love could be mine.

And you make me a better man,
Because I know your love is real.
I place your love among these things
So you will know just how I feel.

The only three things that I'll ever need;
The things that I hold dear
Are Grace from God, love from you
And an ice cold bottle of beer.

It all comes down to these three things.
In my mind there is no doubt.
Everything else that's in my life is
Something I can live without.

A house on the hill with a swimming pool
Would just be a sign of greed.
Money in the bank and a brand new car
Are things that I don't need.

The only three things that I'll ever need;
The things that I hold dear
Are Grace from God, love from you
And an ice cold bottle of beer.

And God made me to be your man,
So you would know that love is real.
By God's good grace with your good heart,
You will know the way I feel.

And so I propose that we drink a toast
To beer and to God above.
Of all the gifts that I've received,
I treasure most your love.

The only three things that I'll ever need;
The things that I hold dear
Are Grace from God, love from you
And an ice cold bottle of beer.

Why in the Hell Ain't I?

My little gal is
Back home in Dallas
Under that big blue Texas Sky.
I sit here drinking,
And I keep thinking,
Now just why in the Hell ain't I?

A long distance call
Just won't help at all
To ease this pain that's in my heart.
I'll say I love you,
Then she'll say it too,
And we'll still be too far apart.

My little gal is
Back home in Dallas
Under that big blue Texas Sky.
I sit here drinking,
And I keep thinking,
Now just why in the Hell ain't I?

There's nothing to win
In this city of sin
That's worth missing out on her touch.
Not enough wages
In all of Vegas
To be worth even half that much.

The boss told me at this trade show,
I'd learn things to help my career.
But the one thing that I now know
Is how much that I hate it here.
My little gal is
Back home in Dallas
Under that big blue Texas Sky.

I sit here drinking,
And I keep thinking,
Now just why in the Hell ain't I?
Forget the money,
I miss my honey,
I'm going to catch the next flight.

If flight twenty nine
Touches down on time,
I'll be holding my gal tonight.

Standup Bass

I know this band from my homeland
With songs that really suit my taste.
What makes them grand is the girl who stands,
As she plays standup bass.

The singer croons; the keyboard's tuned,
The rest of the band keeps the pace,
But it's her tune that makes me swoon,
As she plays standup bass.

She's five foot two or less it's true
And slender as a pool cue case.
But still my view's on her like glue,
As she plays standup bass.

She has to know I love the show,
Since I'm always in the same space.
I'm at each show on the first row,
As she plays standup bass.

After one concert, I stood there in line,
With a new t-shirt just for her to sign.
She dotted each 'i' with a little heart,
And showed me the smile that sets her apart.

So I took a chance on a real romance;
I asked her to join me on a date.
Then we made plans to go and dance
Without her standup bass.

I held her hand each time we danced,
And then I kissed her pretty face.
Now my golden band is on her left hand
As she plays standup bass.

I'm still in my place in a first row space
Each time my wife plays her standup bass.

No Regrets

They all told me you would leave me.
They knew it all too well.
They said you would never love me,
That you'd put me through Hell.

I can't stand the way it ended,
Can't pretend I'm not sad,
But I don't regret one minute
Of the best years I've had.

If I had a chance once again,
To heed my friends' advice.
I'd love you just like I did then
With no need to think twice.

I can't stand the way it ended,
Can't pretend I'm not sad,
But I won't regret one minute
Of the best years I've had.

For each tear I cry for my loss,
I smile a million times.
If the tears I cry are my costs,
It was worth every dime.

I can't stand the way it ended,
Can't pretend I'm not sad,
But I won't regret one minute
Of the best years I've had.

Victims

I'm a victim
Of my penchant
For making bad choices.
I'm a victim
Cause I listen
To all the wrong voices.

It's also true
That pretty soon,
I'll do it once again.
The Devil speaks
And I get weak;
The crying soon begins.

She's a victim
Of this tension,
Cause her love is too strong.
I tell a lie,
She starts to cry,
She knows that I've gone wrong.

But still she stays;
Won't go away
Cause she loves me too much.
And so I try
To do what's right
And justify her trust.

We're both victims
Of our penchant
For making the wrong choice.
The angels say,
Don't go that way,
But we heed the wrong voice.

She Loves

She's as blue as her bright blue eyes,
Glistening as
She sits and cries,
Even though there is nothing that I wouldn't do.
I'm as sad as her broken heart,
Listening as
She falls apart.
I love her; she loves you.

She says things I can't stand to know,
Revealing the
Pain in her soul.
Although it's the one thing I wish she wouldn't do.
I listen to her fall apart,
Concealing the love in my heart.
I love her; she loves you.

I don't say that I love her so.
I mind my fears,
Can't let her know,
Because it's the one thing that I just shouldn't do.
She cries aloud, I cry inside,
I hide my tears
To save our pride.
I love her; she loves you.

I gently hold her hands in mine.
She looks at me;
Her eyes shine.
She can see that there's nothing that I wouldn't do.
I look into her eyes that glow.
She looks again and we both know.
It's love; she loves me too.

You're as dumb as a man can get,
Leaving a love
You can't forget,
Even though there was nothing that she wouldn't do.
I'm as lucky as you are sad,
Grieving a love
You could have had.
It's love; she loves me too.

Sonnet 242

Too much love may still not be quite enough,
For many lovers, that's all there is, though.
Two lovers with past lives will make things rough,
Like too many chefs making cookie dough.

Too much love may lead to a painful vow;
For whatever you reap, so shall you sow.
Two lover's past lives may hurt each one now.
Like too much stuff that they just should not know.

Too much love may not cause us one more tear,
For our friendship may give us strength to bear
Two people like us working past each fear.
Like two more seamstresses fixing a tear.

I disdain these risks and on bended knee,
I ask you, my love, will you marry me?

Silver Wings

He might drink a little more than he should;
And he says 'I love you' less than he could,
But the way he holds me means everything
As we dance as the band plays Silver Wings.

I know silver wings won't take him away,
And I know that his love is here to stay,
Each time he holds me close and tries to sing
As we dance as the band plays Silver Wings.

He may flirt with a bar maid he finds cute,
And his eyes might wander while our boots scoot.
But I don't wonder why I wear his ring.
As we dance as the band plays Silver Wings.

I know silver wings won't take him away,
And I know that our love is here to stay,
Each time he holds me close, and we both sing
As we dance as the band plays Silver Wings.

PAINFUL HEARTS

If love is a game, somebody has to lose. The poems in this section deal with how people cope with losing a love, or possibly losing a love, or not knowing if they are actually in love any longer or if they ever were in love.

Two Days

I was alone long before the letter came,
But I still thought that I'd hold you again

I'd been without you two years,
Before I got the letter.
Been two days without tears,
So I'm getting better.

But I didn't know so it wasn't the same.
Now that I know I'll never hold you again.

I cried each night for ten years
After I got the letter,
Been two days without tears
So I'm getting better.

Make You Want Me Again

Well, of course I knew, I should not want you
When I saw you wore his ring.
I could not resist, such a tempting kiss;
Your vow did not mean a thing.

One look in your eyes led to my demise.
It was nothing I could fight.
I knew it was wrong, but I was not strong,
So I had to hold you tight.

I fell for an unfaithful girl,
I stole you away from your man.
If I sent you back to his world.
Would that make you want me again?

Can't change an unfaithful woman,
So that won't be part of the plan.
But if I were not your husband,
Would that make you want me again?

When he was your man, you could always plan
Some time to spend in my arms.
Now that you are mine, I'm alone all the time,
Someone else enjoys your charms.

Forbidden treasure brought me such pleasure,
I deserve this pain, its true.
Now that its reversed, this pain is my curse,
My penance for loving you.

I fell for an unfaithful girl;
I stole you away from your man.
If I sent you back to his world,
Would that make you want me again?

Can't change an unfaithful woman,
So that won't be part of the plan.
But if I were not your husband,
Would that make you want me again?

If you only knew the way to be true,
I'd not have tasted your kiss.
I know if you had, that I would be sad,
But not near as bad as this.

Well, of course, I see that you don't love me
Even though you wear my ring.
Though your tempting kiss is something I'll miss,
Our vow does not mean a thing.

I fell for an unfaithful girl;
I stole you away from your man.
If I sent you back to his world.
Would that make you want me again?

Can't change an unfaithful woman,
So that won't be part of the plan.
But if I were not your husband,
Would that make you want me again?

I Just Don't Love You Any More

I still think of you when shopping,
Often forgetting we're apart;
Looking around for little things
That I might buy to touch your heart.

I just don't love you any more.
Absence doesn't make love grow.
But it's still you that I adore,
Even though you chose to go.

I saw a snow globe yesterday,
The kind you always liked to find.
I picked it up and went to pay,
Then I remembered you're not mine.

I just don't love you any more.
We're too apart for love to grow.
But I still love you like before,
You tired of me and chose to go.

The things I liked before we met,
A movie or the football game.
I watch them even since you left,
But somehow it's just not the same.

I just don't love you any more.
Absence doesn't make love grow.
But it's still you that I adore,
Even though you chose to go.

They were the things I liked to do,
But now they just aren't very fun.
They only start me missing you;
Wondering what I could have done.

I just don't love you any more.
We're too apart for love to grow.
But I still love you like before,
You tired of me and chose to go.

Sonnet 42

We were true friends before we were lovers,
And yet, we had no hint of these dangers.
It's bad alone beneath these bedcovers,
And yet far worse is that we are strangers.

We said that we would never be apart;
Together forever, at least as friends.
The tragedy of love which has no start
Is this sad way in which it never ends.

You never said you no longer loved me,
And I never said I no longer loved you.
Our romance died so slowly, so sweetly
That we barely even knew it was through.

To lose a love is sad, but not the end,
It is by far more sad to lose a friend.

Words Unspoken

The first time someone ever broke my heart,
She was a red haired beauty from Duluth
With dancing green eyes and racy red lips
Which never told the truth.

I really tried my best to forgive her
Every time that she told me a lie.
But forgiving does not mean forgetting,
No matter how hard somebody may try.

There are three sure ways that a heart can be broken,
With a lie, with the truth or with words unspoken.
However it happens, one thing remains certain,
No words ever stop the hurtin'.

The Bible tells us all, it's a sin to tell lies,
And the truth can hurt just as badly at times.
But, of the three ways that a heart can be broken,
The hardest is words unspoken.

The last time someone ever broke my heart,
She was a blonde haired beauty from Van Nuys
With sparkling blue eyes and cupid's bow lips,
Which never told me lies.

But her truth hurt me worse than a lie could,
At least a lie I could have just ignored.
But I could do nothing when my lover
Said she's not in love with me anymore.

There are three sure ways that a heart can be broken,
With a lie, with the truth or with words unspoken.
However it happens, one thing remains certain,
No words ever stop the hurtin'.

The Bible tells us all, it's a sin to tell lies,
And the truth can hurt just as badly at times.
But, of the three ways that a heart can be broken,
The hardest is words unspoken.

The one time I ever broke someone's heart,
She was a brown haired beauty from Waco
With trusting brown eyes and soft gentle lips,
Which never hurt a soul.

But I couldn't stay with her forever, and
I never found the words to tell her why.
The aches from my own heart being broken,
Never hurt as much as making her cry.

I bounced back from each heart break that I ever suffered.
But from the one heart I broke, I know I won't recover.

Instead

If I had a dollar for every time you said you loved me,
I could buy myself a loft Uptown in New York City.
But if I get that option what I would wish for instead,
Is a chance to know for certain if you really ever did?

Falls

We can all survive the longest fall.
It's the landing that hurts the most.
I was so high before the fall,
I won't survive hitting the coast.

We can all survive the longest fall.
It's the landing that causes the pain.
I was so high before the fall,
That I won't ever be quite the same.

We can all survive the longest fall.
It's the landing that we don't survive.
I was so high before the fall,
That I can't believe that I'm alive.

Choice

I'll cherish forever our first kiss
And rue to my death our wedding night.
A few short months of wedded bliss
Was followed by decades of fight.

Give me lonely
Over misery,
If I'm allowed to make the choice.
A quiet home,
A silent phone
Are better than your screaming voice

I'll never forget your soft caress
Or forgive you for ruining my life.
Words can't describe the kind of stress,
I got because you were my wife.

Give me lonely
Over misery,
If I'm allowed to have my choice.
A quiet home,
A silent phone
Are better than your screaming voice

I meant it when I said I love you, but now I don't.
I said that I'd love you forever, but no, I won't.

Lament

I don't understand how it hurts so bad,
To lose something I knew I never had.

Although you no longer want me around,
I'm glad I could be there when you were down.

You're back on top now where I don't fit in,
I'll be down here if you need me again.

I know you'd have made it without my help,
I tried to help, but it was for myself.

Each penny spent was worth more than a dime,
But to miss you for long would waste my time.

I'll have memories of the fun we had
To cherish when it doesn't hurt this bad.

Thank you for the many good times we had,
I think of them often and they make me glad.

Hurt

Suck it up! Shake it off!
Rub on a little dirt.
Part of the price you pay,
Is having to play hurt.

These words have been passed on,
From coaches and fathers, too,
To their players and sons.
Who often think they're true.

To play the game you love,
You have to play with pain.
It's always been that way;
It will always be the same.

He thinks of those words now,
Although these games are new.
Each time that she hurts him,
He wonders if they're true.

Again, he sucks it up;
Wipes the blood from his shirt.
Part of the price he pays,
Is having to play hurt.

She hurts the one she loves,
And causes him such pain.
However long he stays,
It will always be the same.

Barbie Doll

You say that I'm a Barbie® doll,
Because I don't have a heart at all.
Of course, I never show my heart
To men who might tear it apart.

I've done that one too many times.
That, is pain I hide.
If you could see when my tears fall,
You'd never call me Barbie® doll!

You say that I'm a Barbie® doll,
Because I don't show my heart to all.
Of course, your friends won't see me cry.
When I step out I always try

To hide the pain I feel inside.
Then, I cry all night.
If you could see when my tears fall,
You'd never call me Barbie® doll!

You're back there tending bar five nights every week,
Making nasty comments every time you speak
About all the girls here that you don't really know.
You're the only one who can't see it's all a show.

You say that I'm a Barbie® doll,
Because you don't know my heart at all.
Of course, I talk and smile and dance
And play my part the best I can.

To keep inside the pain I feel.
That, I swear is real.
If you could see when my tears fall,
You'd never call me Barbie® doll!

A Barbie® doll can smile for years,
If I'm a doll, I'm Tiny Tears®.

Wishes

I wish I could take back
So many things I've said.
And I wish I could say
So much I left unsaid.

I wish you still loved me,
Or could at least pretend.
But I know that you don't
And never will again.

I wish I could forget,
So much that I recall.
But that's not how life works.
So I live with it all.

I wish you still loved me,
Or could at least pretend.
But I know that you don't
And never will again.

I wish that I could quit
Loving you like I do.
But if somehow I could,
I would miss loving you.

Brand New Man

I changed because of you,
Like you wanted me to.
I don't stay out all night,
Just looking for a fight.
I gave up booze and smokes.
I don't tell dirty jokes.
Yes, darling, it's a fact.
That I've cleaned up my act.

You only loved who you thought I could be.
So you changed me to someone brand new.
Though I thank you for the ways you changed me,
This brand new man don't love that same old you!

You said to be thinking
About all my drinking.
So I thought it over,
And now I'm cold sober
You said I should try school
And quit being a fool.
So I got a degree,
Then a P.H.D.

You only loved who you thought I could be.
So you changed me to someone brand new.
Though I thank you for the ways you changed me,
This brand new man don't love that same old you!

Not smart to change a man,
But you sure had a plan.
You changed my life around,
Just by cutting me down.
You're still the same old girl
Who used to rule my world.
Now are you missing me,
And who I used to be?'

You only loved who you thought I could be.
So you changed me to someone brand new.
Though I thank you for the ways you changed me,
This brand new man don't love that same old you!

Now, I Hate Them

You've always hated thunderstorms.
They make you scared to be alone.
So every time the thunder roared,
You'd need my hand to hold.

Now every time the thunder roars,
It scares me how much I miss you.
You always hated thunderstorms,
And now I hate them too.

You've always hated to slow down.
It drives you mad to drive that slow.
So every time we drove through town,
You'd need my hand to hold.

Now every time I drive though town,
It drives me mad to not hold you.
You always hated slowing down,
And now I hate it too.

You've always hated wind and snow.
It makes you scared to be so cold.
So every time the sleet would blow,
You'd need my hand to hold.

Now every time the sleet does blow,
It scares me how much I miss you.
You always hated wind and snow,
And now I hate them too.

I used to hate your neediness.
It scared me to be needed so.
I never knew how I was blessed
To have your hand to hold.

Now when I hate most anything,
It always makes me think of you.
You always hated many things,
And now I hate them too.

Half an Hour

In half an hour, I can be packed and gone.
It just won't matter who was right or wrong.
If you and I must fight to get along,
I'll be packed and gone.
In half an hour,
I'll be packed and gone

I think that I don't want to walk your line.
I think that you should try to be more kind.
It just won't matter if I'm right or wrong.
I'll be packed and gone.
In half an hour,
I'll be packed and gone.

You think I need to learn to compromise.
You think my words are barely short of lies.
It just won't matter if you're right or wrong.
I'll be packed and gone.
In half an hour,
I'll be packed and gone.

'Only when love and need are one',
Robert Frost said it well.
But if we need to fight to stay in love,
Then love can go to Hell.

In half an hour, I will be packed and gone.
It won't matter then who thinks who is wrong.
If the two of us can't just get along,
I'll be packed and gone.
In half an hour,
I'll be packed and gone.

True

Wing Men do what all wing men do;
Tell nice lies to hook up their crew.
But there's one big drawback to that.
It just ain't true.
Boyfriends do what all boyfriends do,
Like say, 'I will always love you.'
But there's one big drawback to that.
It just ain't true.

Girlfriends do what all girlfriends do,
Like say, 'I will always be true.'
But there's one big drawback to that.
It just ain't true.
Exes do what all exes do,
Like saying, 'It's me, it's not you.'
But there's one big drawback to that.
It just ain't true.

Good Friends do what all good friends do.
Like say, 'She's a whore and a shrew.'
But there's one big drawback to that.
It just ain't true.
They said that I'd be good for you.
You said that you'd always be true.
Then you said it's me, it's not you.
They say you're a whore and a shrew,
But it ain't true.

My heart does what broken hearts do.
It says, 'I'll find somebody new.'
But there's one big drawback to that.
It just ain't true.
I said that I'd always be true.
I said that I'd always love you.
But there's one big drawback to that.
It's all still true.

Don't Lie

Tell your friends what they want to hear
About whatever made us part.
Tell them all whatever you want
About what caused my broken heart.

But please don't lie to anyone,
And tell them that I did not care.
Don't pretend when you needed me,
That even once I wasn't there.

Tell yourself what you need to hear,
That might ease the pain in your heart.
Convince yourself the way you must
That it's my fault that we're apart.

But don't tell sad lies to yourself,
Or pretend that I didn't care.
Don't lie to yourself or pretend,
That you don't know that I'm still there.

PERMANENT ENDINGS

Losing a love always hurts; sometime it hurts more than others. This section contains poems that involve those times when it hurts so bad, it's to die for.

Sonnet 33

I wrote but not of us while I loved you,
And you returned my love in kind to me.
But now these poems are all that I can do.
I numbered each and this is thirty-three.

I wrote twelve just about what I could do
To win you back and how you did me wrong.
And I wrote five that said I don't need you,
Five lies I wrote to keep myself still strong.

I wrote ten more about life with you gone
And how my life is more than love that's lost;
Four more reminding me that life goes on.
But thirty-two revealed to me the cost.

The world and you have no real need for me.
This last tribute to you is thirty-three.

I Loved You, Too

You were in love just with being in love.
I was in love just with being with you.
So whenever you said you were in love,
I would always say that I loved you, too.

But I never believed that you loved me,
Although I wished that I thought it was true.
If I believed what you said so easy,
I'd have believed just that I loved you, too.

But you just loved how love made you happy,
More than my love or the things I would do.
Your lover could have been anybody,
It did not matter if I loved you, too

I knew each day I loved being with you,
How did I not know that I loved you, too?

Three Sinners

Devil didn't make him do it. He can't blame Satan for this one.
The choice was made of his free will, and it can't be undone.
He coveted his neighbor's wife, instead of doing right.
He thought of her every day, and he took her late one night.
Devil didn't make him do it. It was only the path he took.
Repentance must come from the heart, no sin is overlooked.
One day Jesus might forgive him as only our Savior could do.
But that won't make it less a sin,
Or mean there is no penance due.

Devil didn't make her do it. She can't blame Satan for this one.
The choice was made of her free will and it can't be undone.
She broke the vow she made one day, instead of doing right.
She flirted with her man's friend and seduced him one night.
Devil didn't make her do it. It was only the path she took.
Repentance must come from the heart, no sin is overlooked.
One day Jesus might forgive her as only our Savior could do.
But that won't make it less a sin,
Or mean there is no penance due.

There are saints and sinners
And losers and winners.
Cheaters may never win,
But they may cheat again.

Devil didn't make me do it. I can't blame Satan for this one.
The choice was made of my free will and it can't be undone.
They broke the vow she made to me, instead of doing right.
I thought about what they had done, and I shot them that night.
Devil didn't make me do it. I made a call and sealed my fate.
My soul belongs to Jesus now; my life is forfeit to the State.
One day Jesus might forgive me as only our Savior could do.
But that won't make it less a sin,
Or mean there is no penance due.

I Can't Live Without You

I loved you too much is what I believed
To tell you something that might be a lie.
If I loved you that much I now can see,
I should have had the decency to try.

It could not have been wrong to risk a lie
To say what you wanted so much to hear.
Even were it untrue, I should have tried
To say the words that would have eased your fear.

But I said, 'I love you' each day.
I said it, knowing it was true.
But what you needed me to say
Was that I can't live without you.

But that was what I couldn't say,
Not knowing for sure it was true.
But now that we have parted ways,
I know I can't live without you.

Now that it's too late for me to hold you;
Too late for us and far too late for me.
I know that to say it would have been true,
But it took me far too much time to see.

Your new love knows to say all the right things.
Of course, I once knew all the right words, too.
I held them back, too scared of committing,
And now it's too late for me to hold you.

But I said, 'I love you' each day.
I said it, knowing it was true.
But what you needed me to say
Was that I can't live without you.

But that was what I couldn't say;
Not knowing for sure it was true.
But now that we have parted ways,
I know I can't live without you.

Most days I can work and some nights I sleep.
What I do the most is try not to think;
Because to think brings me pain that cuts deep.
These days, all I ever do much is drink.

The pain that hurts worst, that cuts like a knife
Is that living is just not what I do.
To live is to be someone with a life.
I don't live, I just exist without you.

But I said, 'I love you' each day.
I said it, knowing it was true.
But what you needed me to say
Was that I can't live without you.

But that was what I couldn't say;
Not knowing for sure it was true.
But now that we have parted ways,
I know I won't live without you.

Driving

The road goes on forever, but my party's long since ended.
It ended,
When she said goodbye.
I may drive on forever, but my heart just can't be mended,
I'll keep driving, until the day I die.

Driving myself crazy, wondering why you left me.
Driving; to anywhere but here.
Driving there, with one hand on the steering wheel
And one hand on my beer.

One hand on the steering wheel.
One hand on my beer!

Pour me another cup of coffee, like I am a truck driving man.
Driving man,
Since she said goodbye.
I'll have one more cup of coffee, although it's not the best in the land.
I'll keep driving, until the day I die.

Driving myself crazy, wondering why you left me.
Driving; to anywhere but here.
Driving there, with one hand on the steering wheel
And one hand on my beer.

One hand on the steering wheel.
One hand on my beer!

Deep in the heart of Texas, the stars aren't big and bright for me.
Night for me,
Cause she said goodbye.
As I drive across Texas, dark skies are all that I can see.
I'll keep driving, until the day I die.

Driving myself crazy, wondering why she left me.
Driving; to anywhere but here.
Driving there, with one hand on the steering wheel
And one hand on my beer.

One hand on the steering wheel.
One hand on my beer!

Forever

Forever starts out as a promise,
Sometimes it becomes man and wife.
But a vow only lasts while both keep it,
Sometimes there will be a new life.

Then forever becomes alone,
And someone is bound to be sad.
But when alone turns into forever,
That's when things really get bad.

At first, the heartbroken will try
To sometimes force on a smile.
But even that falsehood will fade
After being alone for awhile.

That's when alone becomes lonely,
And life becomes mostly sad.
But when lonely turns into forever,
That's when things really get bad.

Good friends will do all that they can
To bring cheer and to make it okay.
But sadness spreads easy and deeply,
So they eventually all drift away.

That's when the lonely are forsaken,
To live a life that is always sad.
But when forsaken becomes forever,
That's when things really get bad.

Somewhere between 'too soon now'
And 'too late after all these years'
Are many a night filled with sadness,
That make up a lifetime of tears.

Then forsaken becomes forgotten,
And things are bound to get bad.
When forgotten turns into buried,
The mourners are bound to be sad.

Love Letter

We're not lovers.
We were never lovers.
I love you
Too much to find another.

I see you cry.
I can't help you not cry.
It kills me.
Your tears make me want to die.

You're not my girl.
You'll never be my girl.
I know this,
Yet still you're my whole world.

I am your friend.
I know I'm just your friend.
It hurts me,
But I'll be yours to the end.

I see you're sad.
You're sadness makes me sad.
But sometimes,
It also makes me mad.

They cause you pain.
Some men only cause pain.
You know that,
But you're drawn to their flame.

I cannot live.
Like this, I cannot live.
When I'm dead,
I hope you will forgive.

You never meant.
I know you never meant.
To kill me,
But that's still how it went.

Hand's on the gun.
My hand is on the gun.
It burns hot,
But now my pain is done.

We're not lovers.
We'll never be lovers.
Goodbye, Love.
I won't have another.

Have To Think

I stumbled home from a long day drinking
And poured myself a drink.
If I pass out before I'm done sinking,
I won't have time to think.

Won't have to think about how I miss you,
Or what I did so wrong.
Won't have to think about how I'd kiss you,
If you just had not gone

Tomorrow, I'll wake from a night sinking,
Wash my face in the sink.
I'll know that soon I need to start drinking,
So I won't have to think.

Won't have to think about how I miss you,
Or what I did so wrong
Won't have to think about how I'd kiss you,
If you just had not gone

One day I know that I will quit sinking,
And I won't need a drink.
That will be the day that I stop thinking,
Cause I'll be dead, I think.

Just a Man

The day you stole the heart that stole my heart,
You said you hoped I'd understand.
You never meant to hurt me,
But sometimes a man is just a man.

The night you broke the heart that broke my heart,
You said you hoped she'd understand.
You never meant to hurt her,
But sometimes a man is just a man.

The day she took her life with that damn knife,
I did begin to understand.
You never meant to hurt us,
But sometimes a man is just a man.

That night I took your life with that same knife,
I do hope that you understand.
I never meant to hurt you,
But sometimes a man is just a man.

Now while the firing squad sends me to God,
My parents try to understand.
I never meant to hurt them,
But sometimes a man is just a man.

Happy Endings

He's tall, dark and handsome and his smile's disarming,
So she's starting to believe that he's Prince Charming.
But before she starts planning out their perfect life,
She should ask why Cinderella is not his wife!

You can never have the 'ever'
In 'happily ever after'.
Just try to smile, at least awhile
And enjoy the love and laughter.

In this whole world of boys and girls,
There is love, then hurt, then mending.
Yes, there are joys for girls and boys,
But there are no happy endings.

Her green eyes and soft drawl make him dream of Tara,
So he's starting to think she's Scarlett O'Hara.
But before he starts planning to be her new man,
He should ask why Rhett Butler doesn't give a damn!

You can never have the 'ever'
In 'happily ever after'.
Just try to smile, at least awhile
And enjoy the love and laughter.

In this whole world of boys and girls,
There is love, then hurt, then mending.
Yes, there are joys for girls and boys,
But there are no happy endings.

If you have luck and find a love,
Who is worth the time you're spending,
Don't make things rough by thinking love
Has to have a happy ending.

She dreamt about a knight upon a great, white steed,
And he arrived one day and swept her off her feet.
The perfect pair; true love they shared, for fifty years.
But then he died, and then she cried, unending tears.

You can never have the 'ever'
In 'happily ever after'.
Just try to smile, at least awhile
And enjoy the love and laughter.

Love can be just with one we trust,
But it can't be never-ending.
Each one of us will turn to dust;
That's the only certain ending.

Acknowledgements

I'd like to thank all my friends and loved ones who encouraged me to keep writing and accepted the time I devoted to my writing at their expense. In particular, I'd like to thank those who inspired me to keep improving either by their honest criticism or by their unwavering, if often unwarranted, appreciation of my writing.

I'd also like to thank everybody who has inspired a poem by a casual comment such as, "I sometimes get lonely, but I'm never miserable." or "I had to call a cab because I couldn't find my car." Without your inspiration, my poetry might still be little more than diary entries.

I should also thank and apologize to every stranger, friend and lover who has told me about their lives and now find parts of it repeated within these pages. I should have warned you that when you share your life with a poet, you may end up in a poem one day.

To you all, I promise to keep writing and to keep improving. I also promise to never tell a soul which role your life story played in which poem that I've written unless you want me to do so.